Why Is the Sun So Bright?

by Helen Orme

Gareth Stevens Publishing
A WORLD ALMANAC EDUCATION GROUP COMPANY

Please visit our web site at: www.garethstevens.com
For a free color catalog describing Gareth Stevens Publishing's list of
high-quality books and multimedia programs, call 1-800-542-2595 (USA)
or 1-800-387-3178 (Canada). Gareth Stevens Publishing's fax: (414) 332-3567.

Library of Congress Cataloging-in-Publication Data

Orme, Helen.
    Why is the sun so bright? / by Helen Orme.
       p. cm. — (What? Where? Why?)
    Includes index.
    Summary: Simple text and pictures explain the characteristics of the nine planets
of our solar system, the sun, and the moon.
    ISBN 0-8368-3792-4 (lib. bdg.)
    1. Solar system—Juvenile literature. [1. Solar system.] I. Title. II. Series.
QB501.3.O76   2003
523.2—dc21
                                                        2003045715

This North American edition first published in 2004 by
Gareth Stevens Publishing
A World Almanac Education Group Company
330 West Olive Street, Suite 100
Milwaukee, Wisconsin 53212 USA

Original copyright © 2003 by ticktock Entertainment Ltd. First published in Great Britain in 2003
by ticktock Media Ltd., Unit 2, Orchard Business Centre, North Farm Road, Tunbridge Wells,
Kent, TN2 3XF, England. This U.S. edition copyright © 2004 by Gareth Stevens, Inc.

Gareth Stevens series editor: Dorothy L. Gibbs
Gareth Stevens cover design: Melissa Valuch

Picture Credits
(Abbreviations: (t) top, (b) bottom, (c) center, (l) left, (r) right)
Alamy Images: front cover, pages 4(br), 7(cl, tr), 8(bl), 9(br), 12(cl), 15(r), 16(tl), 17(cr).
Creatas: page 19(cr).
NASA: pages 2(all), 3(all), 4(bl, cl, cr), 5(tl), 6(cr), 8(tl), 9(t), 10(tl), 12(tl, br), 13(tr, cl, cr), 14(all),
15(tl), 16(tr, br), 17(tl, cl), 18(tl, cr), 19(bl, tc, tl), 20(cr), 21(tr, c, b), 22(all), 23(tr, bl, br), 24(all).

Every effort has been made to trace the copyright holders for the pictures used in this book.
We apologize in advance for any unintentional omissions and would be pleased to insert the
appropriate acknowledgements in any subsequent edition.

With thanks to: Lorna Cowan; Robert Massey at the Royal Observatory in Greenwich, England;
and Elizabeth Wiggans.

Printed in Hong Kong

1 2 3 4 5 6 7 8 9 07 06 05 04 03

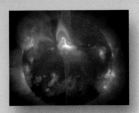

CONTENTS

Words in the glossary are
printed in **boldface** type the first
time they appear in the text.

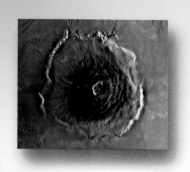

What do you see
when you look at
the night sky?

4

Moon

planets

solar system

You might see a big shining object called the Moon. You might see lots of bright little lights called **stars**. You might even see some larger bright objects called **planets**. The Moon, the planets, and one very important star called the Sun make up the **solar system**. All of the planets in the solar system **orbit** the Sun.

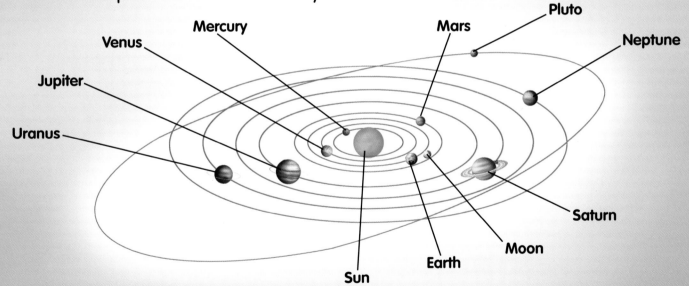

Have you ever wondered how many planets are
in the solar system, or what the planets look like?
Have you ever wondered why the Sun is so bright?

Why is the Sun so bright?

The Sun is a small star.

A star makes light and heat by turning **hydrogen gas** into **helium gas**.

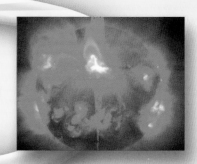

Without the Sun, Earth would always be dark and freezing cold. No plants or people or other animals could live on this planet.

The Sun gives the warmth living things need to grow.

People enjoy the warmth of the Sun when they sunbathe.

Although the Sun is far away from Earth, its heat is so powerful it can burn you if you stay in it too long.

How long would it take to walk to the Sun?

(answer on page 23)

REMEMBER
Never look directly at the Sun. Its light can blind you.

The Sun is the center of the solar system. All the other planets travel around it.

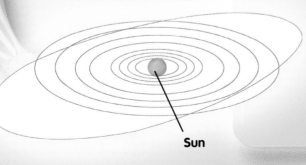

Sun

Which planets are closest to the Sun?

a) Mercury and Venus

b) Mars

c) Earth

(Turn the page to find out.)

Which planets are closest to the Sun?

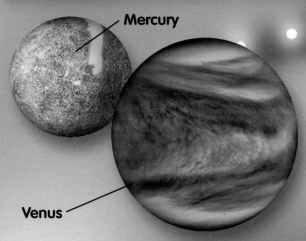

Mercury

Venus

Mercury is the planet closest to the Sun.

Do you think you could live on Mercury?

(answer on page 23)

It is also one of the smallest planets in the solar system.

Mercury

Venus

Mercury is so hot that metal would melt on its **surface**.

8

Venus is the second planet from the Sun. It is also very, very hot.

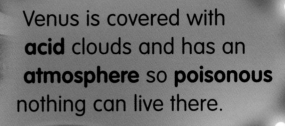

Venus is covered with **acid** clouds and has an **atmosphere** so **poisonous** nothing can live there.

Venus is the closest planet to Earth.

With a telescope, you can take a good look at Venus.

If you look at the sky early in the morning, you can see Venus rising before the Sun comes up.

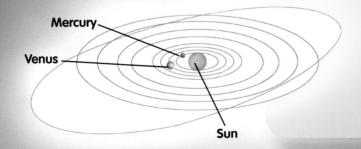

Mercury

Venus

Sun

Which planet is a good place to live?

a) Mars

b) Earth

c) Jupiter

(Turn the page to find out.)

9

Why is Earth a good place to live?

Earth is not too hot or too cold, and it is not covered with clouds of poisonous gas.

Earth is the only planet we know of where plants and people and other animals can live.

A lot of Earth's surface is covered with water. All living things need water to drink.

Earth also has enough **oxygen** for people and other animals to breathe.

Some places on Earth are very hot. A rain forest is very hot.

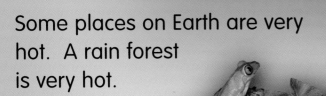

Some places are very cold. **Antarctica** is very cold.

Why is Earth such a good place to live?

(answer on page 23)

Earth is just right for all types of life — from the tiniest snail to the biggest elephant!

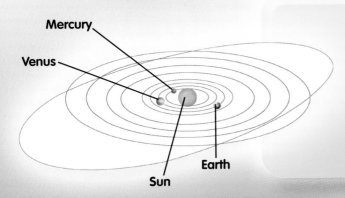

Mercury

Venus

Sun

Earth

Which *object* in the night *sky* changes shape?

a) the Milky Way

b) the Sun

c) the Moon

(Turn the page to find out.)

Why does the Moon change shape?

The Moon is always circling Earth.

It makes one trip around Earth in a month.

During each month, half of the Moon is lit by the Sun, and half is in **shadow**. Depending on where the Moon is, different amounts of its face are lit by the Sun, so the Moon appears to be changing shape.

We know a lot about the Moon because **space probes** and other **spacecrafts** have visited it.

In what spacecraft do modern astronauts fly to the Moon?

(answer on page 23)

The Moon has no weather, no water, and no air.

When **astronauts** visited the Moon, they had to wear special space suits that could help them breathe.

The surface of the Moon is covered with holes called **craters**. Craters are made when lumps of rock from space hit the Moon.

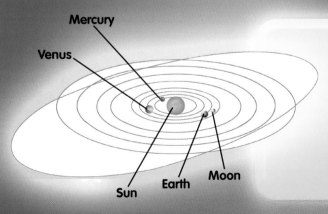

Mercury

Venus

Sun   Earth   Moon

Which planet is called the Red Planet?

a) Earth

b) Pluto

c) Mars

(Turn the page to find out.)

Why is Mars called the Red Planet?

When you see Mars through a **telescope**, it looks red.

It does not look red because it is hot. Mars looks red because it has very red soil.

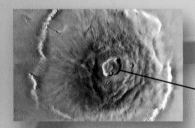

volcano on Mars

Even though Mars is smaller than Earth, it has two moons and the biggest **volcano** in the solar system.

No astronaut has ever gone to Mars, but spacecrafts have visited the planet.

It takes a spacecraft about six months to reach Mars from Earth.

Scientists know that Mars has frozen water on it.

Scientists also think they have found **fossil bacteria** on rocks from Mars, so there might once have been life on the Red Planet.

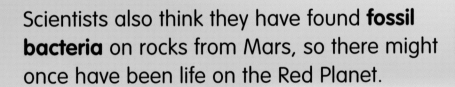

Do you think Mars ever had life on it?

(answer on page 23)

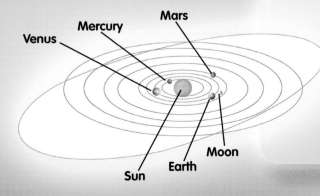

Mars

Mercury

Venus

Moon

Earth

Sun

Which planets in the solar system are the largest?

a) Jupiter and Saturn

b) Mercury and Venus

c) Neptune and Uranus

(Turn the page to find out.)

Which planets are the largest?

The solar system has four giant planets.

Jupiter and Saturn are the two largest.

They both shine brightly and are easy to see, even without a telescope.

Saturn is famous for its rings. They are made of dust, ice, and pieces of rock.

Jupiter is the largest planet in the solar system.

It is twice as large as all the other planets put together.

Through a powerful telescope, you can see that Jupiter is surrounded by bands of **gas**.

How many rings does Saturn have?

(answer on page 23)

red spot

Jupiter also has a giant red spot, which is actually a huge storm that has been blowing for years.

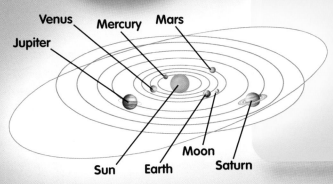

Venus Mercury Mars
Jupiter
Sun Earth Moon Saturn

Which planets are the farthest from the Sun?

a) Neptune and Pluto

b) Mercury and Venus

c) Jupiter and Saturn

(Turn the page to find out.)

17

Which planets are farthest from the Sun?

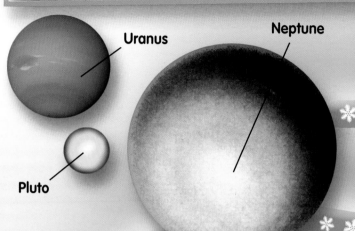

Uranus

Neptune

Pluto

Uranus, Neptune, and Pluto are far, far away from the Sun.

Pluto

Neptune

Uranus

Because they are so far from the Sun, the Sun's light is too weak to warm them up very much.

Uranus, Neptune, and Pluto are icy planets that are colder than the coldest place on Earth.

How cold do you think it is on Pluto?

(answer on page 23)

Space probes have flown past Neptune and Uranus to find out more about them.

These planets have violent storms. A storm spot, like the red spot on Jupiter, has been seen on Neptune.

Neptune's storm spot

Pluto is the planet farthest from the Sun. It is so far away we do not know much about it.

A space probe called New Horizons will visit Pluto in 2015 to find out more.

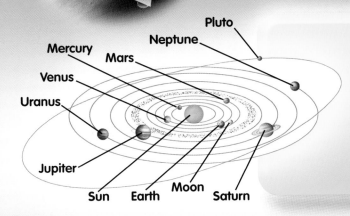

Pluto
Neptune
Mercury
Mars
Venus
Uranus
Jupiter
Sun   Earth   Moon   Saturn

What is outside the solar system?

a) nothing

b) stars and space rocks

c) other planets

(Turn the page to find out.)

What is deep space?

Deep space is everything in the **universe** beyond Earth.

Inside our solar system, deep space includes planets as well as pieces of loose rock. The pieces of rock that fall to Earth are called **meteorites**.

Sometimes, much bigger rocks called **asteroids** crash into Earth. An asteroid made this huge crater.

Deep space does not end with our solar system. We are just a tiny part of a **galaxy** called the Milky Way, which is one of many galaxies.

Scientists have been investigating beyond our solar system.

In 1990, NASA launched the Hubble Space Telescope, which can see far out into space.

Scientists have also sent space probes to photograph stars we cannot see from Earth.

How many probes have been sent into space?

(answer on page 23)

In case the probes make contact with other life-forms, some of them carry discs that will tell listeners about our planet.

THE
SOUNDS
OF
EARTH

UNITED STATES OF AMERICA
PLANET EARTH

GLOSSARY

acid: a chemical substance that can burn or eat away organic tissues, such as skin, and many other materials.

Antarctica: the frozen continent at Earth's South Pole.

asteroids: space rocks that are the size of small planets.

astronauts: specially trained people who travel in space.

atmosphere: the air that surrounds a planet.

craters: large, bowl-shaped hollows or holes, usually made by an explosion or the impact of a huge, heavy object.

deep space: the part of the universe that goes far beyond Earth's solar system.

fossil bacteria: the remains of tiny organisms that lived in an earlier time and became embedded in rock.

galaxy: a huge group of stars.

gas: a colorless and odorless substance that is not a solid or a liquid and will expand to fill any open space.

helium gas: a very lightweight gas that does not burn. A balloon filled with helium will float away in the air if it is not held down.

hydrogen gas: a lightweight gas that burns very easily. To make energy, the Sun turns hydrogen into helium.

meteorites: chunks of rock that break off of asteroids and fall to Earth.

orbit: (v) to move around an object in space in a set, and usually circular, path.

oxygen: a gas in Earth's atmosphere that people and other animals must breathe to stay alive.

planets: ball-shaped bodies of rock or gas, in space, that orbit a star, such as the Sun.

poisonous: dangerous or deadly to eat, drink, or breathe.

shadow: the dark area that is created when an object blocks out light.

solar system: a term used to refer to the Sun, or any other star, along with the planets, moons, and other heavenly bodies orbiting around it.

space probes: spacecrafts that are sent to explore the universe but do not have any people in them.

spacecrafts: vehicles that are specially built for space travel and exploration.

stars: large balls of burning gas that are far off in space.

surface: the outside or top layer of something.

telescope: a device we can look through to make faraway objects appear closer. It is a long tube equipped with carefully arranged lenses and mirrors.

universe: everything found in space, including planets, solar systems, and galaxies.

volcano: a mountain with a crater at the top that, at times, explodes with melted rock and ashes from deep underground.

Could you answer all the questions? Here are the answers.

page 7: It would take a person almost three thousand years to walk to the Sun!

page 8: You could not live on Mercury. The atmosphere is so poisonous nothing can live there.

page 11: Earth has air to breathe, water to drink, and a perfect range of temperatures for a variety of life-forms.

page 13: Today, astronauts use the Space Shuttle to fly to the Moon.

page 15: Lots of scientists think Mars once might have had life on it. They also think we might be able to build a research station on Mars in the future.

page 17: A Voyager spacecraft that flew past Saturn counted thousands of rings.

page 18: It is so cold on Pluto that your body would freeze solid in less than a minute.

page 21: So far, twenty probes have been sent into space.

INDEX